Real Life

GUIDES

WORKING OUTD

REAL LIFE GUIDES

Practical guides for practical people

In this increasingly sophisticated world the need for manually skilled people to build our homes, cut our hair, fix our boilers, and make our cars go is greater than ever. As things progress, so the level of training and competence required of our skilled manual workers increases.

In this new series of career guides from Trotman, we look in detail at what it takes to train for, get into, and be successful at a wide spectrum of practical careers. The *Real Life Guides* aim to inform and inspire young people and adults alike by providing comprehensive yet hard-hitting and often blunt information about what it takes to succeed in these careers.

Other titles in the series are:

Real Life Guide: The Armed Forces
Real Life Guide: The Beauty Industry
Real Life Guide: Carpentry & Cabinet-Making
Real Life Guide: Catering
Real Life Guide: Construction
Real Life Guide: Electrician
Real Life Guide: Hairdressing
Real Life Guide: The Motor Industry
Real Life Guide: Plumbing
Real Life Guide: The Police Force
Real Life Guide: Retailing
Real Life Guide: Working with Animals and Wildlife
Real Life Guide: Working with Young People

trotman

Real Life

GUIDES

WORKING OUTDOORS

Margaret McAlpine

Real Life Guide to Working Outdoors

This first edition published in 2004 by Trotman and Company Ltd
2 The Green, Richmond, Surrey TW9 1PL

Reprinted 2006

© Trotman Publishing Limited 2004

Editorial and Publishing Team
Author Margaret McAlpine
Editorial Rachel Lockhart, Commissioning Editor; Anya
Wilson, Managing Editor; Bianca Knights, Assistant Editor
Production Ken Ruskin, Head of Pre-press and Production;
James Rudge, Production Artworker
Sales and Marketing Deborah Jones, Head of Sales and
Marketing

Trotman Publishing Board
Managing Director Toby Trotman
Commercial Director Tom Lee
Editorial Director Mina Patria

British Library Cataloguing in Publication Data

A catalogue record for this book is available from the British
Library

ISBN 0 85660 995 1

Typeset by Photoprint, Torquay
Printed and bound in Great Britain by The Cromwell Press,
Trowbridge, Wiltshire

Real Life

GUIDES

CONTENTS

About the author

Margaret McAlpine taught for a number of years in schools and colleges in the Midlands and East Anglia before becoming a journalist. Today she writes for a number of publications and has a particular interest in writing careers material for young people. She has three grown-up children and lives with her husband in Suffolk.

Acknowledgements

The author wishes to thank Lantra for its help and support.

Introduction

What comes into your mind when you think of outdoor or land-based jobs?

If it's pulling up turnips in a muddy field in the pouring rain, or sitting with a flock of sheep in the middle of nowhere while the world goes on without you, think again.

Working outdoors doesn't have to mean working on a farm.

While agricultural jobs are an important part of the industry, the term 'land-based' covers far more than working on a farm.

There are opportunities for work in garden centres, engineering companies, golf courses and leisure complexes, both at home and abroad. Land-based industries in the twenty-first century have a lot to offer ambitious young people who are looking for interesting jobs with prospects for promotion.

One surprising fact is that there are jobs in land-based industries in all parts of the UK, urban as well as rural. This means plenty of opportunities for 'townies' who need the rumble of traffic and a choice of leisure entertainment to feel alive. Just think about the acres of parks, gardens, sports turf and even golf courses in and around towns and cities.

All of these need specialist attention if they are to satisfy the leisure needs of the millions of urban dwellers in the UK.

At the centre of most land-based industries is the concept of sustainable development, which means meeting the needs of today's society without damaging the prospects for future generations. Projects include rural regeneration, to bring life back into those areas of the countryside which lack job opportunities and affordable housing for local people. High on the list of important issues are environmental protection and the search for new ways of stopping or lessening pollution.

DID YOU KNOW?

In the last ten years British farmers have planted more than 6,000 miles of new hedgerows providing homes for birds, animals and insects.

So what could a job in a land-based industry offer you? Are you looking for a specialist job where you use your practical skills in a hands-on way, or a technical job where you are trained to use the latest high-tech machinery? Perhaps you want the sort of experience that would open up the possibility of working abroad or could lead to management opportunities? Whatever plans you have for the future, you could be very surprised at the wide range of career openings on offer in land-based industries.

Over 1.5 million people are employed in around 400,000 land-based businesses in the UK. It is a sector made up of very small businesses, with people working alone as sole traders, in partnerships or employing a small number of people. The average land-based business has 2.5 employees. This means there are opportunities for those enterprising people who want to be their own boss and set up their own business.

Land-based qualifications plus the right kind of experience can lead to jobs abroad.

The jobs covered in this book fall into two groups:

- Land management and protection, which covers work such as:
    Agricultural crops and livestock
    Aquaculture (fish farming)
    Fencing
    Land-based engineering
    Production horticulture (growing plants, trees and flowers commercially)
    Trees and timber
    Forest ranger.
- Environmental industries
    Environmental conservation
    Fisheries management (looking after inland waterways for angling clubs; salmon and trout)
    Game and wildlife management
    Landscaping
        Landscape design
        Sports turf and golf green keeping
        Working on private property, heritage sights and botanical gardens
        Working on commercial grounds, public parks and green spaces.

The great news is that unlike many areas of work in which there are more people looking for jobs than there are vacancies, the land-based industry sector is actually looking to recruit hard-working, ambitious young people. A target has been set to bring in 25,000 new recruits over the next five years. This means high quality education and training schemes are available for the right people, leading to career pathways, to job satisfaction and great prospects.

To find out more about these opportunities, including what the work involves, what training is needed and what prospects are on offer, you need look no further than the pages of this book. In it you will find information about jobs within the land-based sector, the different education and training routes leading to entry into such jobs, and promotion prospects once you are in work.

If you are unsure exactly how much you know about the land-based sector, there is a quiz to test your knowledge. There are case studies of people working in the industry, including the Head Groundsman at Old Trafford, the home of Manchester United Football Club.

Also included in the *Real Life Guide to Working Outdoors* are ways for you to find out more for yourself about particular jobs, including addresses and websites of professional organisations and training providers.

1

TONY SINCLAIR

Success story

Tony Sinclair is Head Groundsman at Manchester United Football Club's Old Trafford ground. A loyal Man U fan from his schooldays, Tony managed to get a work experience post at the club while he was at school, and afterwards wrote a letter asking to be taken on in a training position. Today he is in charge of the pitch at Old Trafford and of two training pitches. He moves in the same circles as footballers who are world-famous names and says, 'At the end of the day they've got their job to do and I have mine'.

WHAT MADE YOU BECOME A GROUNDSMAN?
In the first place I just wanted to get into Man U, because I was such a keen supporter, but I soon became fascinated with the pitch and everything connected with it. When I joined the club I was on the Youth Training Scheme (YTS), which is not unlike today's Apprenticeships. We learned on the job and also went to college on day release.

DO YOU ATTEND EVERY MATCH?
I'm on the touchline for just about every game. We examine the pitch both at half-time and after the game, replacing any turf

I'm on the touchline for just about every game. We examine the pitch both at half-time and after the game, replacing any turf that has been kicked up and noting any repairs that need to be done.

that has been kicked up and noting any repairs that need to be done.

IS THE PITCH A MUDDY MESS AFTER SOME MATCHES?
You don't often see a pitch that is waterlogged and muddy these days. This is because pitches today are very sophisticated and designed to withstand play during bad weather. They are usually constructed on a sand base, which drains quickly and efficiently.

Under the Old Trafford pitch are heating pipes, fuelled from a gas boiler to prevent the ground freezing however low the temperature. A system of drainage pipes is also in place to make sure the pitch doesn't become waterlogged or flooded during wet spells. These pipes are laid onto grit and covered with a layer of coarse sand, on top of which is a layer of Rootzone which is a type of sandy mixture. This is topped with a layer of fibre sand mixed with polypropyline to provide stability.

The turf comes in its own layer of sand, which is laid on top of the layer of fibre sand already on the pitch. Laying sand on sand means that the turf settles quickly.

ISN'T THERE A WORRY THAT PLAYERS MIGHT KICK THROUGH THE EARTH TO THE PIPES BELOW?
No you'd need a JCB digger, not a human foot, to dig down so far.

DO ALL CLUBS HAVE SUCH SOPHISTICATED PITCHES?
They do if they can afford them, although the cost of such systems is high, which means they are often too expensive for clubs in the lower divisions.

HOW OFTEN IS A PITCH REPLACED?

We aim to make a pitch last for more than one season if possible and we managed this at Man U in 2003. A great deal depends on the weather and how many matches during a season are played in the rain, which is just a matter of luck. A club might have reasonable weather for its games throughout a season, or be unfortunate and play games in the rain for weeks on end.

HOW DO YOU REPLACE A PITCH?

The next Man U pitch is only a phone call away. It has been growing peacefully in Lincolnshire for the past seven months and is visited regularly by ground staff from the club, to check all is going well. Growing pitches in this way means a minimum of upheaval at replacement time.

DO YOU HAVE A TIME OF YEAR THAT IS PARTICULARLY BUSY?

There isn't one period that is busier than any other. During the season, when matches are played once or even twice a week, there is the regular maintenance of the pitch. During this time the grass is not growing, or is growing very little, so it does not require a great deal of cutting.

During the summer months the grass grows rapidly, which can mean cutting is needed every day. In June and July the pitch is recreated if necessary so there is time for it to settle and for roots to go down before the season begins. My job is an all-year-round one and doesn't finish with the end of the football season.

DOES MANCHESTER UNITED STILL TAKE TRAINEES?

Yes we still take on Apprentices, and their training involves both on-the-job learning and time spent at college.

DID YOU KNOW?

Manchester United Football Club was founded in 1878 when a group of men from the Lancashire and Yorkshire Railway got together to play soccer on Sunday afternoons and became known as the Manchester Heathens. In 1892 the club joined the Football League and in 1902 adopted the now famous red and white colours and became known as Manchester United.

Today Man U is reported to be the richest soccer club in the world. It was the first football club to become a listed company and is supported by about 50 million fans worldwide.

DO YOU STILL SUPPORT MAN U?
Of course!

A landscaping career could involve a job such as Tony's, caring for a famous football pitch, or it could mean keeping a golf course in prime condition, working in a city park or on a historic garden.

To find out more turn to Chapter 4 'What are the jobs?' and Chapter 7 'Training day'.

What's the story?

2

There's no concealing the fact: British agriculture has not had a good time in recent years. Accounts of BSE and foot-and-mouth disease, tales of bankruptcy and near disaster have filled the newspapers and left no one in doubt about the state of farming in the UK.

You might well wonder, then, why you should consider working in such a beleaguered sector. However, agriculture is by no means the only land-based industry, and the prospects for British farming may not be as dire as they appear at first glance.

Some good news is that the government has realised what a valuable resource it has in its land-based industries, and between 2001 and 2006 the Department for Environment, Food and Rural Affairs (DEFRA) is supporting the industry through the England Rural Development Programme (ERDP). Similar support packages are running in Northern Ireland, Scotland and Wales.

DID YOU KNOW?

UK farming contributes £6.6 billion a year to the economy and uses three-quarters of the country's land area.

The ERDP is worth £1.6 billion and so far support has included:

- Over 54,000 training days to improve the skills of people working in forestry and farming through the Vocational Training Scheme.
- The creation or support of over 7,800 jobs through the Rural Enterprise Scheme which assists the development of diversification projects. These have ranged from projects offering help in marketing agricultural produce to converting a piggery into a children's nursery.

  A number of Rural Enterprise projects have been aimed at enhancing public access and enjoyment of the countryside, as the fact is faced that tourism is going to play a vital part in the future of land-based industries.
- Management agreements for 320,000 hectares of land under the Countryside Stewardship Scheme have been set up. This is the government's main scheme for conserving and improving the countryside. Under the scheme, farmers receive grants to follow more traditional farming methods that improve the landscape, encourage wildlife and protect historical features.

  Areas under this scheme have seen an increase in bird life, including the stone curlew, the bittern, the lapwing and the green finch. Over 1,000 miles of dry stone walls and 9,000 miles of hedgerow have been restored. In areas of intensive farming, over 16,000 miles of grass margins have been established to protect hedgerows and the plants and wildlife within them from the effects of crop sprays.
- The conversion of 98,078 hectares of land to organic production methods under the Organic Farming Schemes has been approved.
- The Environmentally Sensitive Areas Scheme is encouraging farmers to help protect areas of the countryside where the landscape, wildlife or historic

interest is of national importance. Under it, farmers enter into ten-year management agreements with DEFRA for which they receive an annual payment.

● The Energy Crops Scheme helps farmers to grow energy crops such as eucalyptus, which can be used to produce heat or electricity, to be used instead of fossil fuels and help to reduce greenhouse gas emissions.

Not only do such programmes conserve and improve the countryside, they lead to the creation of more land-based jobs and improved training for people working in these jobs – and that could be you.

The role of tourism in the land-based sector is set to grow as the countryside becomes more inviting and the public are encouraged to find out more for themselves about rural life. This could mean good opportunities for people who have good communication skills and enjoy sharing their love of the country with others.

With the emphasis on conservation and the need to protect the environment comes a new attitude towards the land. The interests of future generations will have to be weighed against the profit motive, and those working the land will need to understand long-term damage is no longer acceptable for short-term gain. This calls for a new generation of people eager to combine the traditional with the new.

To find out more about the wide range of work available in the land-based sector, turn to Chapter 4 'What are the jobs?'.

THE QUESTION IS 'ARE THEY WORKING?'

If you're cynical, you may wonder exactly what good all these projects are doing for land-based industries in the UK.

While there's still a long way to go, there are definite signs that a more thoughtful approach to the rural environment is having a positive effect – and that has to be good news for anyone considering work in a land-based industry.

Tests reveal that river water quality is improving and that the wild bird population is increasing. Timber production has risen by 10 per cent and sustainable practices are reducing soil damage and threats to wildlife. This means new job opportunities are going hand-in-hand with consideration for the environment.

Agricultural practices are also improving as a growing number of farmers have slurry and manure analysed in a laboratory before spreading it on their land, and fit devices on their machinery to avoid the spread of fertilisers into ditches and hedgerow bottoms.

Fish farming is a growth industry, bringing healthy meals of trout and salmon within the reach of ordinary families. In the early days fish farms were simply places where fish were bred to re-stock rivers. The big breakthrough came when it was realised that when fresh water ran

DID YOU KNOW?

Water voles were once common throughout most of the UK, along riverbanks, ditches and lakes. Between 1990 and 1998 the numbers dropped by 88 per cent as their habitat was destroyed.

Steps are now being taken to restore river banks and other areas where water voles live, in order to save this tiny animal from extinction in the UK.

through the fish ponds the quality of the fish improved and disease levels fell.

The first commercial fish farm opened in Lincolnshire in 1950. Today there are 360 trout farms in the UK, producing 16,000 tonnes of fish a year and providing a great many jobs.

While organic foods remain more expensive than other foods, public interest in them is growing. This is largely because food scares such as BSE have made traceability a buzzword, as customers want to know exactly where their meat came from before it reached their plates. In France, butchers commonly put up notices in their shops giving details of the farms where the meat they are selling that week was reared.

One way buyers can assure themselves of the traceability of their purchases is by buying at farmers' markets, which are held across the country, not only in small market towns, but in urban settings including central London. As people become more concerned about what they eat, so organic farming spreads, with more and more land being approved for organic production.

Jobs and career opportunities in land-based industries may be on the increase, but would they be right for you? That's a difficult question to answer, because the jobs themselves are so varied. The qualities needed for an engineer are different from those for a landscape designer, forester or gamekeeper. It's probably fair to say that so varied is the work that there is something for almost everybody.

Case study

Hugh Fearnley-Whittingstall was born in London and grew up in Gloucestershire. From a young age, he was interested in cookery, although after studying at Oxford University he travelled to Africa to do conservation work. On his return he became a sous-chef at the River Café, but had to leave because his work was so messy. His television career began with programmes such as *TV Dinners* and *Cook on the Wild Side*, which used many ingredients to be found living and growing in the wild.

He is one of an increasing number of people who enjoy eating meat from animals that have been reared in good conditions or have lived in the wild. He does not take kindly to TV viewers who, while eating ham sandwiches from pigs reared in factories, complain about him shooting squirrels and rabbits.

Hugh Fearnley-Whittingstall now lives in a cottage in Dorset where he tries to be as self-sufficient as possible. He has made two TV programmes about his life at River Cottage and has received awards for his work in increasing understanding of quality food and drink in the UK.

While few people become as famous as Hugh Fearnley-Whittingstall, he is typical of the growing number who have a realistic view of wildlife and the countryside and who want to eat good quality produce, which could be the way forward for many farmers today.

Similarly there are a wide range of education and training opportunities leading to careers in land-based industries, including university degrees, HNDs, National Vocational Qualifications (NVQs) (Scottish Vocational Qualifications (SVQs) in Scotland) and Apprenticeships.

A rough guide to wages in land-based industries is as follows, although it is important to remember that pay rates may vary in different areas and with different employers.

DID YOU KNOW?

Apprenticeships are available in the land-based sector and offer a chance to gain high-level skills, qualifications and experience while earning a wage.

- A farm worker can earn around £18,500 a year.
- A forestry worker can earn around £15,000 a year.
- A fish farm employee can earn around £14,500 a year.
- A park ranger with experience can earn around £18,000 a year.
- Managers working in a land-based industry can expect to earn £30,000 and upwards.

To find out more about training and job opportunities turn to Chapter 7 'Training day'.

One aspect of a land-based career which is likely to appeal to the more adventurous is the opportunity for self-employment. It is an area where small businesses thrive and where determination and hard work really can lead to success.

Quiz

How much do you know about land-based industries in the UK? Try out your knowledge and then check your answers.

1. Winter wheat is:

   A. wheat that is harvested in December?
   B. wheat that is planted in winter, but harvested in summer?
   C. wheat imported from Russia?

2. Which of the following trees are conifers:

   A. larch?
   B. pine?
   C. oak?

3. Soft fruit is:

   A. fruit that is over-ripe?
   B. fruit that is small and easily bruised, such as strawberries and raspberries?
   C. fruit grown for sale in large supermarkets?

4. Charcoal is made from:

   A. burning wood?
   B. burning oil?
   C. burning plastic?

5. Coppicing is:

   A. a way of cutting or pruning trees and shrubs to ground level to produce new growth?

B. a way of growing vegetables commercially in greenhouses?

C. a traditional method of ploughing?

6. Margarine is made from:

A. cream?

B. vegetable oils?

C. yoghurt?

7. Which of the following is not grown on UK farms:

A. rice?

B. oats?

C. barley?

8. Which fruit is grown commercially in the UK:

A. cherries?

B. kiwi fruit?

C. bananas?

9. UK National Parks belong to:

A. the Queen?

B. the government?

C. different landowners?

10. Free range eggs are:

A. eggs imported from abroad?

B. eggs laid by hens that are allowed some freedom of movement?

C. eggs from hens that are intensively reared in special cages?

ANSWERS

1. B. Winter wheat is planted from September through December. It sprouts before freezing occurs, then lies dormant underground until the soil warms up in the spring. The wheat grows and matures and is harvested around early July.

Winter wheat has a high content of protein and gluten and is often used for yeast breads. Durum is the hardest wheat and is primarily used for making pasta.

Wheat was originally a wild grass and first grew in the Middle East nearly 10,000 years ago. It was the Egyptians who discovered how to make yeast-leavened breads between 2,000 and 3,000 BC. Since wheat is the only grain with enough gluten to make a raised loaf of bread, it quickly became more popular than other cereals such as oats, millet, rice, and barley.

The workers who built the Pyramids in Egypt were paid in bread.

2. A and B. Both the larch and the pine are conifers. This means they bear fruit in the form of cones and have needle-shaped or scale-like leaves.

Most conifers are evergreens, which means they do not shed their leaves at a certain time of year. However, this is not true of all conifers. The larch is a conifer but it is not evergreen, while the holly is evergreen but is not a conifer because it does not produce cones.

Wood from conifers is known in the timber trade as softwood and is generally softer than wood from deciduous trees which shed their leaves. However yew, which is a softwood, is harder than most hardwoods, and balsa, which is a hardwood, is actually very soft!

3. B. Soft fruits are small fruits without stones such as strawberries, raspberries, blackberries and loganberries.

Today an increasing number of soft fruits are grown in polytunnels which protect the fruit, reduce the need for pesticides and lengthen the time the fruit is available.

4. A. Charcoal is produced by burning or charring wood at a very slow, controlled rate so that the combustion is not completed and the wood does not turn to ash.

The production of charcoal goes back to prehistoric days. Its importance lay in the fact that no other combustible substance generated the heat necessary for the forging of metals.

DID YOU KNOW?

It takes more than two million flowers to make one pound of honey and a honey bee visits between 50 and 100 flowers during one collection trip.

In 1735 Abraham Darby succeeded in making 'coke' from pit-coal and the charcoal industry began to decline.

Today there is a steadily increasing demand for British charcoal for use with barbecues, because it is generally of a far higher quality than imported charcoal.

5. A. Coppicing is the oldest form of woodland management. Most trees re-grow from the base if they are

cut down and will produce a re-growth of young shoots. Thousands of years ago it was recognised that the re-growth of certain trees had particular uses, such as willow twigs for basket making and large poles of oak for timber framing.

After World War II, traditional coppicing began to die out and copses were left to grow wild. Recently there has been a small revival in traditional woodland crafts and coppice skills.

6. B. Margarine is made from vegetable fats and was invented by a Frenchman, Mège-Mouriés, around 1869 in response to a request from Napoleon III who was worried that food shortages could be a major problem for his army.

7. A. The UK climate is not suitable for rice cultivation, which needs both warmth and moisture. It takes three to six months for a rice plant to reach maturity, and an average of 5,000 litres of water to produce each kilogram of rice.

Rice is eaten by nearly half the entire world population, and many countries in Asia are completely dependent on rice as a staple food. The four major rice exporters are Thailand, Vietnam, India and the USA.

8. A. Cherries make up 5 per cent of the UK fruit market, with 88 per cent of production based in south-east England.

9. C. Unlike national parks in many other countries, UK parks are not owned by the government. They are areas of outstanding beauty where the protection of the landscape has been recognised as a priority. Yet within these areas land and homes are owned by the local population.

10. B. For eggs to be classed as free range, there needs to be at least an acre of field for every 400 laying hens. Almost one in four of the hens on British farms is free range.

Were you surprised by your score? No need to take it too seriously, but if you surprised yourself by knowing more than you realised, it could be an indication of an interest in land-based careers. So read on.

What are the jobs?

4

Within the land-based sector there are many different jobs offering different sorts of work. Working outdoors covers a vast range of opportunities from the practical to the highly academic, for people of different ages and abilities.

If you are drawn to outdoor work, if you are serious about your career and are reliable and hard working, there is almost certainly an opening for you.

What follows is a very brief overview of some (but not all) jobs in the land-based sector.

LAND MANAGEMENT AND PRODUCTION JOBS

AGRICULTURE

This is the land-based industry that probably springs to mind when anyone thinks about working outdoors. Agriculture is the production and management of food crops. These vary from hill farms in Wales rearing sheep, to large mechanised arable farms in East Anglia.

Main farm types include:

- dairy
- beef
- sheep
- pigs
- poultry
- vegetables
- cereals
- root crops
- non-food crops such as flax, hemp, lavender, pharmaceuticals and energy crops.

Pharmaceutical crops are those grown for sale to the pharmaceutical industry which uses certain parts of the plant in the production of drugs.

Energy crops are grown to replace fossil fuels, such as coal, in the production of energy such as electricity. Crops include willow, poplar, hemp, straw and miscanthus, a type of grass.

Many farms rather than concentrating on one crop are mixed, growing crops and keeping livestock.

There are good opportunities in the agricultural industry to specialise in an area of particular interest such as livestock management, responsibility for crops or the maintenance of agricultural machinery.

Of the entire UK land area, 74 per cent is under agricultural production and there are an estimated 235,500 farm businesses in the UK, employing approximately 418,000 people.

AQUACULTURE

This is the breeding and rearing of fish (usually shellfish, salmon and trout) for sale to the wholesale or retail trade and, in the case of salmon and trout, to restock rivers and lakes to give anglers better sport.

Fish farms keep stock in cages which are lowered into water. This way the growth of the fish can be monitored and there is no problem catching stock.

The work includes:

- maintenance of equipment and cages
- making sure the fish are healthy
- checking that rearing takes place in good conditions
- keeping stock safe and protected from poachers.

There are around 1,150 fish farms in the UK, employing over 7,000 people.

FENCING

A fence can be simple or high-tech, made of wire, wood, concrete or metal. It can be purely functional or extremely decorative. The different types of fencing include:

- motorway barriers
- sports ground barriers
- institution perimeter fencing
- zoo and animal enclosures

- agriculture, forestry and garden boundary fencing
- security fencing to reduce vandalism
- sound reduction fencing.

The fencing industry is made up of around 15,800 businesses employing 47,500 people. Businesses range from large commercial companies to self-employed contractors. Anyone thinking of setting up their own business could find fencing a very good option.

LAND-BASED OR AGRICULTURAL ENGINEERING

This involves putting scientific, technical and engineering knowledge to use solving agricultural problems, and working with different types of agricultural machinery – from tractors to sprayers and harvesters.

Job opportunities cover:

- design and development work
- testing machinery by using it on farms
- working for a manufacturing company making machines
- selling machinery
- carrying out repairs and servicing
- contract work (carrying out work on farms, using high-tech machinery.

There are almost 6,000 land-based engineering businesses in the UK,

DID YOU KNOW?

The invention of the seed drill in 1701 by Jethro Tull was a big step forward for British agriculture. Previously seeds were thrown onto the ground randomly, which was wasteful. The drill distributed seed into ploughed furrows by using a rotating cylinder. Modern drilling machines may be much more sophisticated, but they obey the same principle as Jethro Tull's first drilling machine.

The development of agricultural machinery has changed farming from a labour-intensive industry to a high-tech operation.

employing 28,000 people. In addition, more than 3,000 mechanics work independently on agricultural machinery.

FORESTRY, ARBORICULTURE AND TIMBER PROCESSING

What's the difference?

Forestry is the management of woodlands and forests, while arboriculture is the cultivation of trees and shrubs in areas such as car parks, gardens and grass verges. Together they make up the forestry sector of land-based industries.

Forestry work includes:

- establishing conifer plantations for timber production
- creating woodland of broad-leaved trees for game management
- raising seedlings in forest nurseries.

Arboriculture covers:

- establishing new trees
- carrying out tree surgery operations to make sure trees look good and stay healthy
- designing landscaping schemes
- carrying out contracts for tree care and tree planting.

Timber processing involves:

- marking timber
- measuring
- sawing
- transportation.

Greenwood trades cover traditional crafts such as coppicing and charcoal production.

There are around 6,200 businesses employing more than 31,000 people in this industry. It is a popular area of employment, so there is competition for jobs.

PRODUCTION HORTICULTURE
Horticulture is the large-scale production of plants for food and for ornamental purposes. The term *plant* is a broad one covering fruit, vegetables, herbs, mushrooms, flowers, shrubs and trees.

Gardens are big business. TV programmes showing how to change a wilderness into a horticultural showplace virtually overnight are on screen several times a week.

Homeowners now see an impressive garden as an important selling point, in the same way as a modern kitchen or up-to-date bathroom. Production horticulture caters for everyone from the occasional gardener who wants to put in the minimum of effort to the serious professional.

Retail selling operations include:

● garden centres
● nurseries
● farm shops
● pick-your-own centres.

DID YOU KNOW?

One of the tallest softwood trees in the world is the General Sherman, a giant redwood sequoia in California. It is around 275 feet high and measures 25 feet around the trunk.

As well as growing and selling the plants there are opportunities to work in research and technology areas such as:

- hydroponics – growing plants without soil
- automatic watering.

In the UK there are around 13,000 businesses ranging from small private nurseries to large production organisations and together employing 70,000 people.

ENVIRONMENTAL INDUSTRIES

ENVIRONMENTAL CONSERVATION
This is about making the best use of scientific knowledge to produce solutions which meet the needs of both today and tomorrow. The key word is *sustainability* – making sure that decisions taken today consider the long-term well-being of the planet. This includes the protection of rural and urban landscapes, plants and animals, rivers, coastal zones and waterways.

There are jobs at local level on projects such as recycling, and at national level, for example protecting areas of outstanding national beauty, while international issues such as global warming are bringing together countries across the world.

There are almost 5,000 organisations working in the environmental sector in the UK, employing around 56,000 people. It is

DID YOU KNOW?

East Anglia is the largest horticultural producing region in the UK, followed by the East Midlands and particularly Lincolnshire and then the south east of England, especially Kent.

estimated that this number is swelled by around 200,000 volunteers.

Jobs in environmental conservation are becoming increasingly popular, so there is growing competition for jobs. Gaining experience through voluntary work is one way of making yourself more appealing to employers.

PARK AND COUNTRYSIDE RANGERS

These look after areas of countryside set aside for visitors such as country parks. Their work includes

- managing and maintaining the area
- educating visitors – giving talks and keeping visitor centres up to date
- protecting the area from vandals
- taking responsibility for the safety of visitors.

FISHERIES MANAGEMENT

Angling is one of the most popular sports in the UK. Every weekend, anglers of all ages can be seen waiting patiently on river banks and lakesides for that moment when a fish takes their bait.

Angling is not just a relaxing pastime. Over £3 billion a year is spent by anglers on their sport, creating over 12,000 full-time jobs. These include:

DID YOU KNOW?

In 1949 the National Parks and Access to the Countryside Act paved the way for the creation of national parks in England and Wales.

Between 1951 and 1957 ten national parks were confirmed: the Brecon Beacons, Pembrokeshire coast, Snowdonia, Dartmoor, Exmoor, the Lake District, Northumberland, North York Moors, the Peak District and the Yorkshire Dales.

In 1989 The Norfolk and Suffolk Broads were added to the list and in 1999 the South Downs and the New Forest.

- working for angling clubs and syndicates
- making sure waters and banks are well stocked, kept in good condition and not over-fished
- employment in fishery trusts researching diseases that affect fish.

GAMEKEEPING AND WILDLIFE MANAGEMENT

This includes the management of wildlife habitats and populations such as deer, grouse and water birds.

It can involve the breeding and rearing of game birds such as pheasant and partridge, which are then released into the wild, ready for the shooting season.

Aspects of the work include:

- maintaining wild habitats, buildings and pens
- checking on the health of the wildlife
- protecting them from predators such as foxes
- managing sporting estates and keeping them in good order
- preparing and running shoots for guests and visitors.

Around 5,000 game and wildlife businesses are operating in the UK. While some employ full-time gamekeepers, other staff have a dual role combining gamekeeping duties with other jobs on an estate.

LANDSCAPING
This is the design, planning, creation and maintenance of designed landscapes, both rural and urban. These include sports turf, golf courses, parks, historic and domestic gardens and leisure facilities.

The landscape industry is made up of almost 38,000 businesses employing around 112,000 people. Employment opportunities range from self-employment to jobs with local authorities.

5

A day in the life

Robert Adams works as a gamekeeper on a private estate in Essex. He is 18 years old and has just completed a two-year apprenticeship. During this time he spent a day a week at Otley College of Agriculture and Horticulture.

'My day begins early and by 7am I am at work and checking the partridge, pheasants and ducks in the rearing pens. Once I know all is well, I feed the birds and change their water.

'I then move on to the task of the day, which varies according to the season. It could be getting new pens ready or moving straw for the birds. We also construct straw rides in the woods. This involves laying down straw to form paths for the birds and sprinkling wheat down so they have to scratch for it. Once the birds have matured they are set free from the rearing pens and find their own food, usually from the rides we have set up for them.

I also enjoy the environmental aspect of my work. Gamekeeper do a great deal of conservation work. It is not true that all we're interested in is shooting birds.

'Shoots are held on the estate between September and February. These are days when paying or invited guests come to the estate to shoot birds. Guests bring their own guns and draw lots for which peg they stand on. The birds are fed at a set time of day so we have a good idea of where they are.

'Around 10am the guns arrive and then the beaters are sent out to disturb the ground around the rides, by banging their sticks against the undergrowth. This makes the birds fly up into the air and when this happens the guests take aim with their guns.

'Many guests take home birds at the end of the shoot, but there are always dead birds left on the ground which have to be picked up during the day. Some of these are given to the beaters and the rest are sold to dealers who sell game.

'The shoots stop in February so the birds can breed and the young can be reared undisturbed. Our first task is to catch the laying stock and bring them into the pens. This is not an easy task because at that time of year the weather is usually dreadful and we are battling against snow and rain to make sure the birds have a plentiful supply of food.

'The birds are caught in traps baited with food and then they are transported to the pens. These have electric fences to keep out prey such as foxes which can be a major problem. Not a lot can be done to stop them attacking birds in the wild, but at least while they are in the pens we can try to keep them safe.'

WHAT DO YOU PARTICULARLY LIKE ABOUT YOUR JOB?
'I love the fact that no two days are ever the same. It's not at
all like being in an office, doing the same type of job day
after day. That's not to say that on bitterly cold days when
I'm outside, I don't look forward to coming indoors.

'I also enjoy the environmental aspect of my work. It often
surprises people to learn that gamekeepers do a great deal
of conservation work. It is not true that all we're interested in
is shooting birds. Our job includes improving the birds'
habitat and protecting the ecosystems needed to make sure
they can thrive.'

**IN YOUR OPINION WHAT TYPE OF PERSON MAKES A GOOD
GAMEKEEPER?**
'Gamekeepers obviously need to be interested in birds and
like working outdoors. Having said that, I get really annoyed
at the stereotype of the gamekeeper most people believe in.

'First of all, there's the idea that gamekeepers need to be
thick, miserable, solitary types who can't stand living in the
real world and so have to escape into the countryside, with
only their birds for company.

'Gamekeepers come in all shapes and sizes and are
certainly not depressed and moody. By the time careers
were being discussed at school I had become interested in
gamekeeping. We were taken to a careers fair and told to
look into any job that interested us and to find out what it
involved. I found out as much as I could about gamekeeping
that day and then spent my work experience on a game
farm working as part of a team with a head-keeper and
under-keeper.

'Looking back, I think both my school and college were shocked at my choice of gamekeeping as a career. First I was a townie, not born and bred in the country. This probably made people feel I didn't know what I was doing and had an unrealistic view of the work. Secondly I did well at my GCSEs and could have gone on into the sixth form to take A-levels.

'I feel quite annoyed at these reactions because not everyone wants to follow an academic career, no matter how bright they may be, and gamekeeping is certainly not a job for people who can't do much else.'

WHAT WAS YOUR TRAINING?
'My Apprenticeship lasted for two years and during that time I learned an enormous amount, especially from my head-keeper who knew so much about the job and was happy to share it with me. My only problem with Apprenticeships is the pay, which is almost always very poor.

'I couldn't have survived without the support of my family during that time. They may have been surprised at my career choice, but they've always been there for me. However, I do realise that for many young people an Apprenticeship isn't a possibility because of the low pay.'

WHAT ABOUT THE FUTURE?
'I'm ambitious and want to learn as much as I can. Eventually I'd like to be a head-keeper.

'The pay isn't great, but there are perks that go with the job. Clothing is provided and, during the shooting season, tips from the guns can be good. Some jobs provide accommodation, but at present I'm happy to live at home which is quite close to my work.

'I do worry that if hunting is banned, shooting and fishing will be next in line and I'll be out of a job. Still, it hasn't happened yet and if it does I'll have enjoyed my time as a

As the natural resources they need are used up, the mortality rate of wildlife increases and the birth rate drops. Gamekeepers try to increase the level of wildlife by providing an improved habitat and by increasing food levels. At the same time they aim to reduce the death rate from predators and disease. For these reasons, managed game populations are very productive and often have higher breeding stocks than populations that are not managed and not shot.

It can be argued that game management in the UK has supported environmental conservation in a number of ways. These include:

- the retention of heather moorland for grouse shooting
- the planting of woodland for pheasants
- the management of field margins to help partridge chicks which provide a habitat for wild flowers and butterflies
- the planting of game food crops for game birds, which also provide food for songbirds.

gamekeeper. If I have to start a new career, I'll still have my GCSEs to fall back on.'

There is a great deal more to working as a gamekeeper than organising shoots. If a career in gamekeeping and wildlife management appeals to you, find out more in Chapter 4 'What are the jobs?' and Chapter 7 'Training day'.

Tools of the trade

6

No more fighting your way on to overcrowded trains or buses, an end to sitting in endless traffic jams, a chance to be close to nature and enjoy some peace and quiet.

Described in that way, working outdoors sounds idyllic: new-mown hay, newborn lambs, wild roses in the hedgerows. Given such wonderful settings it's a wonder anyone can bear to work indoors.

DID YOU KNOW?

There are twice as many farm animals in the world as humans.

The reality is of course different. Working outdoors does not suit everyone. While there are many different types of land-based jobs, suiting a wide range of personalities and interests, there are some qualities that are needed to enjoy an outdoor job and do it well.

- **Working outdoors means exactly that** – five days a week, whatever the weather. The days when the sun is shining and the birds singing as you start work are probably outnumbered by the wet, cold, windy, foggy, miserable days, when at least a couple of layers of extra clothing are needed in order to keep reasonably warm and dry.
- You need to have **a genuine interest in the area in**

which you work, whether it's with animals, plants, machinery or in any other land-based industry. This is essential because animals need feeding and plants need tending whatever the weather and there is not much chance of finding an indoor job to pass the time when it's raining.

Many people take a change in their career and find great enjoyment and satisfaction in working in a land-based industry, but the choice can't be made solely on the desire to escape to the country and leave behind a boring or stressful job.

- It takes **stamina** to work outdoors. The work is often physically demanding and can involve a great deal of effort. To do it well, you need to be fit and to enjoy exercise and activity. Whether you're building fences, field-testing machinery, planting trees or looking after animals, you're likely to feel tired at the end of the day, no matter how physically fit you may be.
- Although working outdoors might appear to free you from the sometimes difficult task of working with other people, this is far from the truth. **Teamwork** is essential in many outdoor jobs because businesses tend to be small and so everyone needs to work well with everyone else.
- Small businesses can bring a great deal of job satisfaction because more often than not you are able to see the end results of your work, rather than working on one small part of a large project. However, you will also need to be **flexible** in your attitude to your work. In small companies, job descriptions tend to be more fluid than in large ones and everyone is expected to pitch in and do whatever is needed.
- Whatever job you do **you will need to be reliable and take your responsibilities seriously**. There is no room

for anyone in any company who comes in late, leaves as early as possible and takes frequent 'sickies'.

This is particularly true of small companies doing work which needs to be carried out to a strict schedule. If animals and plants are not fed and watered, they die. Broken machinery needs to be repaired as quickly as possible, and if customers are let down over deliveries they will find a new supplier. In a small land-based business it is vital that all employees pull their weight.

- Most land-based outdoor jobs demand **practical skills**, although that doesn't mean that quick thinking and common sense are not important as well. Many jobs require a practical approach to problems and a high level of physical dexterity (being good with your hands).
- Working outdoors can mean being responsible for your own daily work plan. You have a list of jobs to be done and it is up to you to make sure that when you finish work your tasks are completed. This is not as simple as it may seem, because when the unexpected happens you need to be able to re-plan your time and prioritise your activities so that the most important tasks are done first and you **meet your deadlines**.

Crops take nutrients out of the soil and, if the same crop is grown for several seasons, soil becomes exhausted and the crop suffers. Farmers working the land as early as 700 BC were aware of this problem and tried to solve it by growing crops on the land one year and grazing animals on it the next.

In the eighteenth century, Viscount Townsend, a landowner and enthusiastic farmer, whose approach to agriculture was definitely hands-on and practical, came up with an answer to soil exhaustion by introducing a new method of crop rotation on his farms. His system covered four years and consisted of growing wheat in the first field, clover (or rye grass) in the second, oats or barley in the third and, in the fourth, turnips or swedes.

This four-field system meant the land was not only rested, but also improved by growing different crops. The clover and turnips grown in a field, after wheat, barley or oats, naturally replaced nutrients into the soil. None of the fields had to be taken out of use in order to recover. Also, where animals grazed on the clover and turnip fields, eating the crop, their droppings helped to manure the soil.

Townsend's enthusiasm for root crops led to his nickname of Turnip Townsend.

7

Training day

Given the wide range of jobs available in the land-based sector, it is only to be expected that there are many different ways of entering the industry. Whether you are academic and enjoy reading, writing and carrying out your own research, or prefer a hands-on and practical approach to learning and training, there is a way in for you.

APPRENTICESHIPS

A popular way of entering a land-based industry is by way of an Apprenticeship. These provide an opportunity to learn while working, and combine practical skills gained in the workplace with theoretical knowledge. The number of Apprenticeships has risen considerably in recent years, from 75,800 in 1997 to over 255,500 today.

The new 'family' of Apprenticeships was launched in June 2004. It comprises:

- **Young Apprenticeships** available for young people aged 14 years, who are still at school. They spend up to two full days a week in the workplace and the rest of the time in the classroom.
- **Apprenticeships** leading to an NVQ Level 2, Core Skills including communication, application of number and information technology and a technical qualification such as a BTEC or City & Guilds.
- **Advanced Apprenticeships** leading to an NVQ Level 3 (equivalent to two good A-levels), Core Skills and a technical qualification.

Similar training opportunities are available in Scotland, Wales and Northern Ireland. Details are to be found on the following websites:

- Scotland – www.scottish-enterprise.com
- Wales – www.elwa.ac.uk
- Northern Ireland – www.delni.gov.uk.

Apprenticeships were once aimed at young people, but now there is no age limit. They are open-ended, which means that each Apprentice completes the course in his or her own time. As a general rule, Apprenticeships take around one to two years and Advanced Apprenticeships two to three years.

Most but not all Apprentices are employed and receive a wage from their employer.

Some employers ask for GCSEs in certain subjects and for particular grades, while others are more interested in the person, their interests and their enthusiasm for the work.

People applying for Apprenticeships may be asked to take a psychometric test, which is a written test giving the employer an idea of a candidate's personality and interests. Literacy and numeracy tests may also be given to measure a candidate's reading, writing and number skills.

Further information about Apprenticeships can be found by visiting your local Connexions office, or on the following websites:

- www.connexions.gov.uk
- www.apprenticeships.org.uk

NATIONAL VOCATIONAL QUALIFICATIONS (NVQS)

These are work-based qualifications gained while doing a job. They are a statement of how well an individual can perform a particular task, and of the knowledge and understanding he or she has in order to perform the job competently.

NVQs are available in England, Wales and Northern Ireland. Scotland has a similar range of qualifications known as Scottish Vocational Qualifications (SVQs).

There are five levels of NVQ (SVQ):

DID YOU KNOW?

There is no longer an age limit on Apprenticeships. They are now open to all age groups.

- Level 1 covers foundation skills in an occupation
- Level 2 builds on these skills to cover the operative skills needed to perform semi-skilled tasks
- Level 3 covers skills at craft, skilled and supervisory levels
- Level 4 covers technical and junior management skills
- Level 5 covers specialist skills leading to chartered or professional status and to senior management positions.

Individuals who have practical experience of doing a particular job can be given credit for the skills they already possess, when working towards an NVQ.

BTEC NATIONAL QUALIFICATIONS

These are vocational qualifications leading to entry into either employment or higher education.

THE BTEC NATIONAL AWARD
This is roughly equivalent to one A-level or an equivalent qualification. It is graded at three levels: pass, merit or distinction (P, M, D).

THE BTEC NATIONAL CERTIFICATE
This is roughly equivalent to two A-levels or equivalent qualifications. The Certificate is double graded, for example, PP, MP, MM.

THE BTEC NATIONAL DIPLOMA
This is roughly equivalent to three A-levels or equivalent qualifications and is triple-graded, for example, PPP, PPM.

BTEC courses are run in land-based subjects across the UK. For further information contact your local college or Connexions office.

NEW DEAL
If you are out of work at the moment, New Deal could offer you the help and support you need to find a new job.

On the programme you will be given a personal advisor who will get to know you and understand your experiences, interests and goals and help you prepare a plan of action for your future.

New Deal offers help to people of all ages from 18 years to 50 plus.

To find out more go to the New Deal website at www.newdeal.co.uk

DID YOU KNOW?

An early form of on-the-job training was offered by guilds in the Middle Ages. Apprentices, who were almost always boys, could be as young as 12 years old when their parents paid for them to be taught a trade by a guild member.

During an apprenticeship, which could last up to 14 years, apprentices lived with their masters. During this time they were expected not to get married or to drink in pubs.

Once an apprenticeship was over, the young person became a journeyman and was paid a wage. Once a journeyman had saved enough money, he could start up his own business.

Lantra

This is the sector skills council for land-based industries. On its website www.lantra.co.uk you will find information about careers, education and training including colleges and training providers across the UK.

DEGREE LEVEL

The days are gone when the only way to university was sixth form and A-levels. Today universities welcome mature students who bring with them life and work experiences which are in their own way just as valuable as UCAS points.

FOUNDATION DEGREES

These are relatively new arrivals on the academic scene. Employers are involved in the way they are designed, and they aim to meet skill shortages at higher technician level.

Foundation degrees are offered by universities working with higher and further education colleges, which means courses are often available locally.

Flexible study methods such as distance learning, weekend and evening classes are specially designed to suit people in work, unemployed people and those wanting to work towards a career change.

A full-time foundation degree course takes around two years to complete, and a part-time course lasts between three and four years.

Foundation degree graduates often already have a job. They can go on to take a professional qualification or to study for an honours degree (which takes a further 12 months of full-time study, or longer if studied part time).

There are no set entry requirements for a foundation degree; offers of places are made by the university or college running the course. Often experience gained from work in a particular job is taken into consideration.

Foundation degrees are run by universities and colleges in just about every area of the UK. The following is just a small sample of such courses:

- Agriculture
- Horticulture
- Arboriculture
- Landscape and Garden Design
- Turf Grass Science and Technology
- Animal Husbandry and Management
- Organic Farm Business Development
- Landscape Management
- Fish Farming and Fishery Management
- Hill Farming
- Game and Wildlife Management.

BACHELOR OR FIRST DEGREES
Some colleges and universities run these courses on a part-time or distance learning basis.

When studied full time, a degree course usually lasts for three years, or four years in Scotland. Some courses offer students an opportunity to take a year out working in an approved job connected with the degree course. Although doing this means studies take longer, the benefits gained from such work experience can be enormous. They can result in a more impressive class of degree as students bring real-life experience to theoretical situations, and can be a great asset when looking for a job because employers look for hands-on experience as well as academic qualifications.

Some universities and colleges ask for particular A-level grades or equivalent qualifications, while others are more flexible, judge each application on its own merit and are prepared to consider experience as well as academic achievement. The Universities and Colleges Admissions Service (UCAS) website, www.ucas.com, provides a wealth of information about degree courses in the UK and the universities and colleges running them, together with entry requirements and weblinks to the colleges themselves.

Degrees were once considered to be the height of purely academic achievement. Today many degree courses combine theory with practical, hands-on experience. The choice of degrees is immense and includes:

- Agricultural Technology
- Mechanical Agriculture
- Crop Science
- Rural Resource Management
- Soil Science
- Sport Fishing
- Fishery Biology

- Landscape Architecture
- Organic Horticulture
- Sport Turf Science.

ACCESS COURSES

These aim to encourage adults, and people from non-traditional backgrounds, who would benefit from a university education but lack the necessary qualifications, to prepare for admission to a degree course.

Anyone over 19 years is eligible to apply, and increasing numbers of undergraduates enter university via Access courses. Information on Access courses can be found on the UCAS website.

MASTER'S OR SECOND DEGREES

Some undergraduates take a first degree in an academic subject that interests them, such as geography, history, politics, English or sociology, and then go on to study for a second degree or a diploma in a specialist area leading more directly to employment.

This is an excellent way of enjoying study for its own sake, if the money is available. The downside is that it adds significantly to the already high cost of a degree. Some Master's courses are run on a part-time basis or by distance learning, which makes it possible to have a job and study at the same time.

Postgraduate diploma courses usually last for an academic year (September to June). Postgraduate degree courses include the writing of a dissertation which is usually submitted the September after the course commenced.

Proceed with caution! Graduates going into land-based industries are in a good position to move into management level jobs, but this is by no means certain to happen.

Gaining a degree is a costly business. A first degree costs around £12,000 and this figure is not going to get any lower as universities adjust tuition fees to cover their costs.

Unless you are fabulously wealthy or have parents happy to support you for years, do your research thoroughly before applying for a place on a degree course.

If you're not sure what you want to do, where or why you want to do it, there could be a lot to be said for gaining some practical experience before you make such a big commitment of time and money.

access to

LAND BASED INDUSTRIES

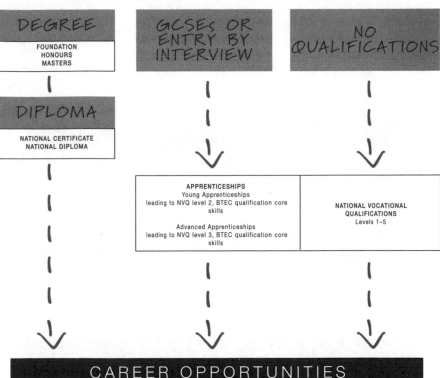

DEGREE	GCSEs OR ENTRY BY INTERVIEW	NO QUALIFICATIONS
FOUNDATION HONOURS MASTERS		

DIPLOMA

NATIONAL CERTIFICATE
NATIONAL DIPLOMA

APPRENTICESHIPS
Young Apprenticeships
leading to NVQ level 2, BTEC qualification core skills

Advanced Apprenticeships
leading to NVQ level 3, BTEC qualification core skills

NATIONAL VOCATIONAL QUALIFICATIONS
Levels 1–5

CAREER OPPORTUNITIES

DEVELOPMENT OPTIONS

MANAGEMENT ✦ SELF-EMPLOYMENT

NATIONAL VOCATIONAL QUALIFICATIONS (NVQs)
SCOTTISH VOCATIONAL QUALIFACATIONS (SVQs)

WORK-BASED QUALIFICATIONS, OPEN TO PEOPLE OF ALL AGES, WHILE DOING A JOB

LEVEL 1

FOUNDATION SKILLS

LEVEL 2

SEMI-SKILLED TASKS

LEVEL 3

CRAFT, SKILLED AND SUPERVISORY TASKS

LEVEL 4

TECHNICAL, JUNIOR MANAGEMENT SKILLS

LEVEL 5

SPECIALIST SKILLS LEADING TO CHARTERED PROFESSIONAL STATUS
AND SENIOR MANAGEMENT POSITIONS

8

Possible problem areas

PHYSICAL ACTIVITY

Many jobs in the land-based industry involve a great deal of physical work and can include bending, lifting and carrying. This may not be suitable for someone who has back problems.

OUTDOOR WORK

For some people there is nothing like working outdoors. Whatever the weather, they would rather be in the open air than in a factory or an office. However, the outdoor life isn't for everyone.

The British climate gives us far more dull dark days than sunny ones. In recent years, freezing winters have given way to warmer, wetter ones, but nobody knows how long this will continue and a murky, muddy miserable day is much less pleasant than a bitterly cold, bright one.

You may enjoy walking and relaxing outdoors, but this doesn't mean you would enjoy working in the open whatever the weather. To do so demands a fair degree

DID YOU KNOW?

If you value your long Bank Holiday weekends, the UK is not the best place to live. Our eight Bank Holidays a year are fewer than those of any other European country except Holland, which has seven. Top of the league is Italy with 16!

DID YOU KNOW?

Typically, it rains on about one day in three in England and more often in winter, although most years do see long dry spells.

The Lake District and the western Highlands of Scotland are among the wettest areas of the country, with average annual rainfall exceeding 2,000 mm. The Pennines and the moors of south-west England are almost as wet. The sunniest parts of the UK are along the south coast of England, where many places achieve annual average figures of around 1,750 hours of sunshine. The dullest parts of England are the mountainous areas, with less than 1,000 hours of sunshine a year.

of self-discipline and a good state of physical health.

DECISION-MAKING

Although you are likely to be working as part of a team, you will need to act on your own initiative and make your own decisions. If you find this daunting and prefer to take instructions from somebody else, you could find yourself having problems.

FLEXIBILITY

Everyone needs a life outside work – time to spend with family and friends and to enjoy hobbies and interests. Having said that, a land-based job may bring with it less regular leisure hours than other areas of work. Certain times of year are busier than others and when problems arise, this can mean extra hours at work. This is true of any job, but because of the number of small businesses in the land-based sector, such incidents are likely to happen more frequently.

If it is important for you to work regular hours and to leave work on time, think carefully before seeking a job in the land-based sector.

Getting a job

9

Before applying for jobs, there are some questions you need to think about.

- Where do you want to live?
- Are you prepared to relocate or do you need to stay in the same area?
- If you are happy to move, in which areas would you prefer to work?
- Are there any areas which you would not consider?

Bear in mind that you might need to be flexible about location if you are to find the job you want.

FINDING JOBS

Job vacancies are often advertised in the local and national press, on websites and in specialist magazines and journals.

The *Guardian* newspaper has an environmental jobs supplement on a Wednesday.
Environmental vacancies can be found on www.green4u.co.uk
Local government jobs can be found on www.lgjobs.com
The Forestry Commission carries details of its own vacancies on www.forestry.gov.uk

The following publications are among the many that carry job advertisements:

AGRICULTURE
Farmers' Weekly
Farming News
Farming Life
Scottish Farmer

FISH FARMING
Fish Farmer
Fish Farming International

HORTICULTURE
The Grower
Horticulture Week

APPLYING FOR JOBS

Once you start applying for jobs, it's important to be organised and to keep details of jobs for which you have applied, dates of application and final results. It's quite normal to be disappointed when rejections drop through the letterbox, but this happens to everyone.

A good way of dealing with disappointment is to keep job applications flowing. This way there's always something else in the pipeline. It's also worth thinking about why you are being unsuccessful. Do you lack work experience? Would time spent observing people doing the job help your applications? Are you presenting yourself as positively as possible?

Always apply for a job in the way requested in the advertisement. If you are asked to send a covering letter and a CV, do exactly that. If the advertisement says send a letter of application including particular details, that is what you must do. Don't be tempted to send a CV with a brief note if time is short and all the necessary information seems to be in the CV anyway. Check the information requested in the job advertisement and make sure you have covered everything.

CVs
Have you got one and if so does it do you justice?

A CV is a summary of your training, education, employment and interests. It should be brief enough to be read quickly and should be laid out in a way that makes it easy to follow. There is no set style or format for a CV, but it should be well written. Grammar and spelling mistakes create a very bad first impression.

You might consider putting the most important information first, such as qualifications gained, courses taken, work experience and previous employment, then moving on to education, hobbies, etc.

If your CV is on a computer, don't be afraid to move information around and add details so your CV shows your particular skills and experience in relation to each job for which you apply.

APPLICATION FORMS
A good tip is to photocopy these as soon as you receive them and then rehearse by filling in the copy. This way you can avoid

DID YOU KNOW?

The curriculum vitae, or CV, began life in academic circles as a summary of an individual's teaching and research experience, their published works and the presentations they had given.

Today a CV is a useful tool for any job seeker.

having to cross out and erase information in the original, which remains clean and uncreased.

LETTERS

It used to be thought that letters should be written by hand, while CVs were printed. Today, when so many people use PCs, it is quite acceptable to print both.

Some employers ask for a letter of application, instead of or as well as a CV. In that case, you have to describe your education, training, work experience and employment in such a way that they show how well suited you would be for the job you want. These letters need to be well planned and carefully written and this takes time. While it is possible to adapt the core information in such a letter to different job applications, it is not a good idea to use the same letter for every job.

A covering letter sent with a CV should be a brief affair. Set it out as a business letter and simply say that you wish to apply for a certain job, which was advertised on a particular date in a named newspaper or journal and that you include either a copy of your CV or a completed application form with the letter.

Although a letter is an opportunity to stamp your own personality and stand out from the crowd, it doesn't pay to be too clever. Jokes can fall flat, and remember the person dealing with your application is likely to be very busy. Rather than being witty and different, it's probably best to concentrate on providing well-written, well-presented information, giving a clear picture of yourself and your skills and interests.

COPING WITH AN INTERVIEW

It arrives at last – the invitation to an interview.

The best advice for an interview is to be yourself, but the best 'yourself' possible. There's no point in pretending to be someone you're not, because even if you could keep up the pretence for the interview, you couldn't keep it up for years in a job.

Prepare for the interview by finding out as much as you can about the job you will be doing. This could be by searching websites, reading books or talking to people. Nobody will expect you to know everything about the company or the job, but you will be expected to have some background information.

Most important, read through the copy of your application form or letter several times before the interview, to remind yourself of what you said. Answer the questions honestly, stressing that you are willing to learn. Pretending you know something you don't will only lead to difficulties and all too often to embarrassment.

'I once interviewed a girl who took out a sandwich after about ten minutes and asked if she could eat it because she'd had no lunch. I was so shocked I didn't say anything, but she didn't get the job.'

Employer

Don't be afraid to ask questions, but don't feel you have to do so. It could be that everything you want to know is talked over during the interview, and asking questions just for the sake of doing so is a waste of everyone's time and suggests you haven't been listening.

If you're feeling nervous you could get a friend or family member to give you a mock interview. Prepare a list of possible questions and try to answer them as convincingly as possible.

Interview clothes should support the image of a keen, businesslike person rather than be noticed in their own right.

It's not just what you say that interests the interviewer, it's how you act.

Try to keep your hands still, however nervous you feel. Don't be tempted to fiddle with rubber bands, paper clips or any other small object.

Don't keep looking at your watch.

Equally, don't slouch into a chair however comfortable it might be.

Don't slip your shoes off, even if you think they can't be seen under the table.

Make sure everything you wear is clean and neatly pressed and, if there is a choice, go for the formal rather than the flamboyant. Don't wear anything that is likely to distract you from the job in hand. Elaborate hairstyles and tight or uncomfortable shoes or clothes will only take your mind off what really matters.

'Smart but comfortable' are the key words. The last thing you want is to be thinking about how you look. Once you are in an interview, relax and you'll find that in a strange way you may quite enjoy it. Whatever happens, remember, whether you are successful or not, you can gain a great deal of valuable experience from an interview.

FURTHER READING

For more information on CVs and making applications, have a look at the Winning series, published by Trotman (www.trotman.co.uk).

Winning CVs for First-time Job Hunters, 2nd edition, by Kath Houston

Winning Interviews for First-time Job Hunters, by Kath Houston

Winning Job-hunting Strategies for First-time Job Hunters, by Gary Woodward.

10

Making your mind up

Before making a decision about a career there are questions that need to be asked. If you are thinking of a job outdoors either on leaving school or as a career change at a later stage, you need to do your own research. The best way of doing this is by talking to as many people as possible who are working in the type of job that interests you.

Carrying out your own research is particularly important as working outdoors covers such a wide range of jobs that it is difficult to generalise about the industry as a whole. What is true for someone working in dairy farming may not apply at all to a person selling agricultural machinery or specialising in the maintenance of sports turf.

DID YOU KNOW?

Farmers make up 60 per cent of the world's population.

The most important advice is to find yourself practical experience before you make any decisions. Not only does this give you a chance to talk to people who are doing the job, it is by far the best way of knowing whether the job is right for you.

HOW LONG DO I HAVE TO TRAIN?
How long is a piece of string? Qualifications can be gained by taking full-time or part-time courses at a college or

university. Work-based vocational training includes NVQs and SVQs and is available to people of all ages. Apprenticeships offer people an opportunity to gain qualifications while working in a job.

In many cases the length of time taken to gain a qualification is flexible and depends on the individual. Gaining an NVQ Level 1 or Level 2 generally takes around one to two years.

For further information on training for a land-based career, see Chapter 6 'Tools of the trade'.

WILL I HAVE A NORMAL WORKING WEEK?
Probably not, but again it depends on the type of job you are doing. You will be given time off, but in many jobs you will need to be flexible about the hours you work. Animals need to be fed or checked over weekends and Bank Holidays. In many jobs the work is seasonal, with employees working long hours at particular times such as harvest or during the summer fruit season.

Flexibility is the key to many jobs, especially in small firms. Land-based industries are made up largely of companies employing just a few people. If you follow the self-employment route and set up your own company you must be prepared to work long and irregular hours.

WHAT'S THE PAY LIKE?
Pay rates vary across the country and with different employers, so it is impossible to be precise. A rough guide to wages in land-based industries is as follows: rates for farm workers are around £18,500 a year; a forestry worker earns around £15,000 a year; a fish farm employee earns

around £14,500 a year; a park ranger with experience can earn around £18,000 a year. In some cases, accommodation comes with the job, and uniforms or working clothes are provided.

WHAT ABOUT HOLIDAYS?
After 13 weeks in a job, all employees are entitled to paid leave of 20 days every year. As outdoor jobs are often seasonal, with one part of the year being particularly busy, those working in the industry may be required to take their holiday at a certain time, in order to make sure as many people as possible are on hand during busy periods.

CAN I CHANGE CAREERS EASILY?
It depends what job change you have in mind. Some skills are interchangeable between jobs.

DID YOU KNOW?

Research has shown that the UK public is sadly ignorant of the agricultural and horticultural industries. For example a large number of school children questioned recently were unsure of the link between cows and milk.

WHAT DOES THE PUBLIC THINK OF THE INDUSTRY?
While many urban families in European countries such as France have kept up their links with the countryside through relatives who still live and work in rural areas, this is not true of the UK. The Industrial Revolution, which began around 1760 and brought thousands upon thousands of people into the cities to work in factories, has resulted in widespread ignorance of exactly what rural life is about today.

Reading the profiles in this book, you will see that the subjects had no direct experience of working outdoors within the family and that one of them found it difficult to make people take him seriously because he was considered intelligent enough to follow a more academic career.

There are, however, signs of a welcome change. Some areas of work such as sports turf management and landscape design are becoming positively trendy, while there is growing interest in careers in forestry and conservation. Farmers are being encouraged to diversify and efforts are being made to attract visitors to rural areas. As this happens, ignorance and preconceived ideas about living and working in the country are beginning to fade.

Equally important, career satisfaction springs largely from finding the right job for you. Some people might think working on a fish farm or in a garden centre is stranger than working in an office or a garage. Are you going to plan your career around what other people think, or are you going to do your own research into what is right for you?

WHAT ARE THE PROSPECTS FOR PROMOTION?
There are always opportunities for energetic, hard-working individuals to get on. However, there are better prospects in some job areas than in others. For example, while some large farms, fish farms and garden centres do have a promotion structure in place which provides employees with a chance to move up the career ladder, this is not common in smaller concerns. Promotion often means changing jobs.

CAN I WORK ABROAD?
There are some good opportunities to work abroad. UK qualifications are well respected across the world, and the more highly qualified a person is, the greater the chances of finding work.

It's important to remember that the vast majority of the world does not speak English and anyone who is serious about working abroad needs to develop their language skills.

WHAT IF I WANT TO BECOME SELF-EMPLOYED?
This is easier in some areas than in others. There are good openings for mechanics specialising in agricultural machinery and for landscape gardeners to set up their own business. The fact that the land-based industry is made up of so many small companies bears witness to the number of opportunities for self-employment.

However, in some sectors the amount of money needed to set up in business is beyond the reach of most people. For example, farm managers wanting to become farm owners need to buy or lease large areas of land, which is so expensive it is not an option for many.

Anyone considering self-employment needs to develop their business skills. Running your own business involves far more than having a talent for a certain job. Designing superb gardens is fine but, to make a living from it detailed quotes need to be worked out covering labour, materials and expenses. Invoices have to be sent out on time and accounts kept in good order. Self-employed people need to know how to promote themselves and their business and to plan two or three years ahead. This doesn't come naturally, but there is really good professional help out there. A good place to start could be your local Learning Skills Centre or Business Link. For further information see the Resources section at the end of this book.

For more information on self-employment take a look at
Working for Yourself Uncovered by Andi Robertson,
published by Trotman (www.trotman.co.uk).

The rich and famous including royalty have often seen
country life as an escape.

The English King George III had a deep interest in
agriculture and experimented in the gardens around
Kew Palace. Because of his interest, he was
nicknamed Farmer George.

Marie Antoinette, wife of King Louis XVI of France, had
a country retreat built at the Palace of Versailles to
remind her of her childhood days in Austria. She used
to play there at being a milkmaid.

11

MIKE GLOVER

Profile

Mike Glover is Managing Director of Barcham Trees Ltd. Based near Ely in Cambridgeshire, the company is the largest of its type in the UK and specialises in growing trees in containers.

Mike explains:

'The roots of trees grown in traditional black containers coil around each other as they grow. The roots thicken in this position and cannot be straightened out. The result is that when the tree is planted in the ground it never becomes well established and fails to thrive.

'I had come across an Australian container system where trees were planted in white polyethelene containers. This enabled light to reach the roots and encouraged them to grow straight down, while reflecting heat and keeping the root system cool.

'The use of these containers meant that trees could be containerised for longer and still thrive. Today few people want to wait years for a tree to grow. They want to enjoy it immediately and have it form part of a garden design in the same way as flowers.

I love my job and corny as it sounds, if won the lottery tomorrow, I'd still want to carry on working.

'Today Barcham Trees is the largest specialist containerised tree company in Europe, growing trees between 10 feet and 30 feet tall. We grow 350 varieties of trees, most of them deciduous. In a way, we are a horticultural battery farm. We even grow olive trees! Since the arrival of warmer summers in the UK, olives do well in the southern area of the country and particularly in London where the underground transport systems keep the earth warm.

'Around 40 people are employed by Barcham Trees, the majority of them care for the container stock and make sure quality is maintained. We are situated in the Fens, an area known for harsh winds and every year we lose around 500 trees through wind damage. We see this as a natural weeding out process. Our trees need to be hardy and face different types of weather conditions. We don't protect them in polytunnels although we do have our own weather station so we know what type of weather to expect.

'Customers come from all over the UK, Ireland, Germany, Holland and France. We sell to local authorities, contractors and architects who use the trees in supermarkets, hotels, parks and housing developments. Our trees make regular appearances on television gardening programmes such as *Ground Force*.'

HOW DID YOU FIRST BECOME INTERESTED IN HORTICULTURE?

'I'd always enjoyed growing things, but knew practically nothing about land-based careers. I did A-levels and went to university to read economics.

'In the first year I knew I'd made a mistake, but had no idea what to do. My sister sent me an article about careers in horticulture and I applied to Writtle College in Essex to take a Higher National Diploma in Commercial Horticulture. Sensibly the college replied that as I had no practical experience I would need to take a pre-entry year working in the industry.

'I spent 12 months working with a rose grower and I loved it. I learned so much in that year and my time there convinced me that nothing at all can beat practical experience. My course at Writtle College lasted three years and at the end of it I won a scholarship to study instant gardening techniques in California.

'While many people in the UK put in a new kitchen or bathroom when they buy a house, in California they put in a new garden, often spending up to half as much on this as on the house itself. They don't want to wait for five years or longer until their garden is at its best, because by that time they may have moved house again. Homeowners in California want an instant beautiful garden and providing these is big business. While I was there I also happened to witness the successful moving of the largest tree ever, which was quite a sight.

'In the US I realised I wanted to specialise in working with trees, which I see as the backbone of horticultural architecture. On my return to the UK I started trawling for job opportunities and met other people like me, with similar views and ideas. This was the point at which Barcham Trees became available and we felt we could take on the challenge.

'The first ten years were spent fire fighting. There was so much to do we just got on with the job, meeting the need for larger containerised trees. The business grew and last year we potted 65,000 trees in containers.

My advice to everyone interested in horticulture is to get out there and find some practical experience before you commit yourself to anything. It's the only way to know if something is right for you.

'Today as managing director my job is to look at the market, examine trends and consider possible future developments. One of my most important tasks is to keep lines of communication open within the company, so that problems are discussed openly.

'In a company which is developing quickly, job roles change which is why training is important. One of the best things that happened to Barcham Trees was a training grant from DEFRA, which enabled every employee to have training. All of us have gained from this and the benefits to the company have been enormous.'

WOULD YOU RECOMMEND A CAREER IN HORTICULTURE?
'I love my job and corny as it sounds, if I won the lottery tomorrow, I'd still want to carry on working.

'Having said that, there are drawbacks. Horticulture is not the most accessible of careers. All the names of plants and trees are in Latin, which puts a lot of people off from the start.

'A major problem in the horticultural industry, in my opinion, is that the majority of businesses are still family-owned. This means that they are passed on to children or to other family members who may well not be seriously interested in horticulture. The business suffers because it could be run by more enthusiastic people, while young people with real talent and energy are denied the chance to move up in a company and really make a difference.

'For the sake of the industry as a whole, matters can't continue like this for ever, but changes seem to be very slow in coming and meanwhile a lot of talent is being wasted.

- Trees not only look good, they also benefit the environment.
- A large beech tree provides enough oxygen for the daily requirements of ten people.
- Trees have a positive effect on conditions such as asthma, skin cancer and stress related illness by filtering out polluted air, reducing smog formation, shading out solar radiation and by providing an attractive, calming setting in which to relax.
- They can save up to 10% of energy consumption through their moderation of the local climate.
- They help to lock up the carbon emissions that contribute to global warming.
- They reduce noise in cities by acting as a sound barrier.

'Another problem I have noticed is the decline in the number of sandwich courses and pre-entry years working in the industry. Today many colleges seem to feel the need to take students in and get them through their courses as quickly as possible. My pre-entry year made sure I knew exactly what I was doing before I started my course.

'My advice to everyone interested in horticulture is to get out there and find some practical experience before you commit yourself to anything. It's the only way to know if something is right for you.'

Production horticulture provides great opportunities for those people who enjoy growing things and are interested in using technology to solve problems.

To find out more turn to Chapter 4, 'What are the jobs?' and Chapter 7, 'Training day'.

12

The last word

By this stage you should have a better idea of whether a land-based career is right for you than you did when you picked up the book and started reading.

There are good job opportunities for the right type of person, plus a great deal of job satisfaction. You are the only real judge of whether you are suited to this type of work, and at this stage you may still not be sure.

That is not a bad thing, because this book is a stepping-off point, giving an overview of the industry and the training opportunities within it. There is a great deal more to be learned and considered before committing yourself to a career in a land-based industry.

For anyone who is seriously interested in one of the careers mentioned in this book, a wise step would be to get some work experience. No amount of reading and research can match seeing for yourself exactly what a job involves. If you are already in work, but considering a career change, you might need to consider giving up some holiday time for work experience. However, the long-term benefits will far outweigh the inconvenience.

If after seeing the work for yourself, you remain convinced that a certain job is right for you, the next step is to look at entry options.

Would your present skills and qualifications enable you to move into your chosen job area?

If not, what type of further training would you need?

Are you in a position to take up a full-time training course, or would a part-time option enabling you to earn some money at the same time suit you better?

What about a job with training leading to a vocational qualification?

Whatever questions you have, there is help at hand to find the answers. In the Resources section that follows, there are a great many organisations listed to help you move forward towards an interesting and fulfilling career.

Resources

Listed in this section are contact details for organisations that can give you further information about education and training opportunities and job openings in land-based industries.

GENERAL INFORMATION
Edexcel
Stewart House
32 Russell Square
London
WC1B 5DN
Tel: 0870 240 9800
Website: www.edexcel.org.uk

Information on the website on a wide range of qualifications including BTECs, GCSEs and NVQs.

Connexions
Website: www.connexions.gov.uk

Careers information for young people, with links to local Connexions offices.

Learning and Skills Council
Cheylesmore House
Quinton Road
Coventry
CV1 2WT
Tel: 0845 019 4170
Website: www.lsc.gov.uk

The Learning and Skills Council (LSC) is responsible for funding and planning education and training for over-16-year-olds in England. The website contains details of training opportunities for both youth and adult learners.

In Scotland this work is undertaken by

Scottish Funding Councils for Further and Higher Education
Donaldson House
97 Haymarket Terrace
Edinburgh
EH12 5HD
Tel: 0131 313 6500
Website: www.sfefc.ac.uk

In Wales by

Education and Learning Wales
Tel: 08456 088 066
Website: www.elwa.ac.org.uk

In Northern Ireland by

The Department of Education
Tel: 028 9127 9279
Website: www.deni.gov.uk

Lifelong Learning
Part of DfES (Department for Education and Skills)
Website: www.lifelonglearning.co.uk

Information on the website on Career Development Loans – deferred repayment bank loans to pay for vocational learning or education.

New Deal
Website: www.newdeal.gov.uk
(Part of Department for Work and Pensions)

Website contains information for people claiming benefits on
the help and support available to help them look for work,
including training and job preparation.

UCAS
Website: www.ucas.ac.uk

Information on degree courses in the UK.

**INFORMATION ON TRAINING AND JOB OPPORTUNITIES IN
THE LAND-BASED SECTOR**

Lantra
Lantra House
Stoneleigh Park
Nr Coventry
Warwickshire CV8 2LG
Tel: 0845 707 8007
Website: www.lantra.co.uk

Lantra Wales
Royal Welsh Showground
Llanelwedd
Builth Wells
Powys LD2 3WY
Tel: 01982 552646
Website: www.lantra.co.uk/wales

Lantra Scotland
Newlands
Scone
Perth PH2 6NL
Tel: 01738 553311
Website: www.lantra.co.uk/scotland

Lantra is the Sector Skills Council for the land-based sector. Its website contains a wide range of information on training and job opportunities with useful links to other websites.

Napaeo
The Association for Land Based Colleges
Website: www.napaeo.org.uk

Napaeo is the Association of Further and Higher Education Colleges which have specialist provision in land-based and related subjects. Member colleges deliver full-time, part-time and most forms of flexible learning courses, ranging from pre-entry to postgraduate levels across most of the subject areas. Courses include:

- Agriculture
- Animal Care
- Aquaculture
- Business Management
- Countryside Management
- Environmental Conservation
- Equine Studies
- Floristry
- Food Processing
- Game Conservation

- Horticulture
- Sport and Leisure
- Trees and Timber
- Veterinary Nursing.

INFORMATION ON SPECIFIC JOB AREAS

AGRICULTURE
National Farmers' Union
Agriculture House
164 Shaftesbury Avenue
London WC2H 8HL
Tel: 020 7331 7200
Website: www.nfuonline.com

Website information on farming plus links to some major
agricultural colleges.

Farmers' Union of Wales
Llys Amaeth
Plas Gogerddan
Aberystwyth
Ceredigion SY23 3BT
Tel: 01970 820820
Website: www.fuw.org.uk

NFU Scotland
Head Office
Rural Centre – West Mains
Ingliston
Midlothian EH28 8LT
Tel: 0131 472 4000
Website: www.nfus.org.uk

ENVIRONMENTAL CONSERVATION
Countryside Agency
John Dower House
Crescent Place
Cheltenham GL50 3RA
Tel: 01242 521381
Website: www.countryside.gov.uk

Funded by DEFRA, the Countryside Agency employs 600
countryside specialists and support staff. The website
includes regional job opportunities.

Countryside Council for Wales
Maes-y-Ffynnon
Penrhosgarnedd
Bangor
Gwynedd LL57 2DW
Tel: 0845 1306229
Website: www.ccw.gov.uk

Scottish National Heritage
12 Hope Terrace
Edinburgh EH9 2AS
Tel: 0131 447 4784
Website: www.snh.org.uk

Rural Development Council Northern Ireland
17 Loy Street
Cookstown
Co Tyrone
Northern Ireland BT80 8PZ
Tel: 028 8676 6980
Website: www.rdc.org.uk

FENCING
Fencing Contractors Association
Warren Road
Trellech
Monmouthshire
NP25 4PQ
Tel: 07000 560722
Website: www.fencingcontractors.org

The FCA is a trade association for the fencing industry and is involved in legislation, standards and training.

FISHERIES
Institute of Fisheries Management
22 Rushworth Avenue
West Bridgford
Nottingham NG2 7LF
Tel: 0115 982 2317
Website: www.ifm.org.uk

FORESTRY
Forestry Commission (England)
National Office
Great Eastern House
Tenison Road
Cambridge CB1 2DU
Tel: 01223 314546
Website: www.forestry.gov.uk

Forestry Commission (Scotland)
Silvan House
231 Corstorphine Road
Edinburgh EH12 7AT
Tel: 0131 334 0303

Forestry Commission (Wales)
Victoria House
Victoria Terrace
Aberystwyth
Ceredigion SY23 2DQ
Tel: 01970 625866

The Forestry Commission is the Government department responsible for forestry policy throughout Great Britain. The Secretary of State for Environment, Food and Rural Affairs has responsibility for forestry in England. Scottish Ministers have responsibility for forestry in Scotland, and the Welsh Assembly Government has responsibility for forestry in Wales. The Forestry Commission website includes job opportunities.

Forest Service Northern Ireland
(An agency within the Department of Agriculture and Rural Development)
Forest Service
Dundonald House
Upper Newtonards Road
Belfast BT4 3SB
Tel: 02890 524480
Website: www.forestserviceni.gov.uk

The Arboricultural Association
Ampfield House
Ampfield
Romsey
Hampshire SO51 9PA
Tel: 01794 368717
Website: www.trees.org.uk

Website includes education and training advice plus jobs vacancies.

GAME AND WILDLIFE MANAGEMENT
National Gamekeepers' Organisation Charitable Trust
PO Box 3360
Stourbridge DY7 5YG
Website: www.gamekeeperstrust.org.uk

Website contains careers advice and information on college courses.

National Gamekeepers' Organisation
PO Box 107
Bishop Auckland
DL14 9YW
Tel: 01388 665899
Website: www.nationalgamekeepers.org.uk

Information on gamekeeping on the website, plus sections of National Gamekeepers' magazine online.

HORTICULTURE
Royal Horticultural Society
80 Vincent Square
London SW1P 2PE
Tel: 020 7834 4333
Website: www.rhs.org.uk

Website information on training, exams and horticultural careers.

LAND-BASED ENGINEERING
Institution of Agricultural Engineers
West End Road
Silsoe
Bedford MK45 4DU
Tel: 01525 861096
Website: www.iagre.org

The Institution of Agricultural Engineers (IAgrE) is the professional body for engineers, scientists, technologists and managers in agricultural and land-based industries. The website includes information on qualifications and job vacancies.

LANDSCAPING
British Association of Landscape Industries
Landscape House
Stoneleigh Park
National Agricultural Centre
Warwickshire CV8 2LG
Tel: 02476 690333
Website: www.bali.org.uk
Website information on training and job vacancies.

The Greenkeepers' Training Committee
Aldwark Manor
Aldwark, Alne
York YO61 1UF
Tel: 01347 838640
Website: www.the-gtc.co.uk

Website information on golf course greens, plus useful training links.

INFORMATION ON SELF-EMPLOYMENT
Business Eye in Wales
www.businesseye.org.uk

Business Gateway Scotland
www.bgateway.com

Business Link
www.businesslink.gov.uk

Invest Northern Ireland
www.investni.com

USEFUL BOOKS
Careers 2005, Trotman

Working in Agriculture and Horticulture, Connexions

Working with Animals, Connexions

Working with Animals, Victoria Pybus, Vacation Work

Working with the Environment, Tim Ryder and Deborah
Penrith, Vacation Work